W9-BSX-107

_A_ GIFT FOR

_F_ROM

The paintings in *Shakespeare on Love* are by the Great Masters of the Renaissance period, and the Pre-Raphaelite Movement. The motifs that illustrate the book are taken from engravings of the original ceramic tiles that paved the floors of cathedrals and monasteries in medieval England.

Published simultaneously in 1999 by Exley Publications Ltd in Great Britain, and Exley Publications LLC in the USA. This edition published by Exley Publications Ltd. in Great Britain and supplied to Hallmark under license. All rights reserved. No part of this publication may be reproduced or transmitted in any form or by any means, electronic or mechanical, including photocopy, recording or any information storage and retrieval system without permission in writing from the publisher.

2 4 6 8 10 12 11 9 7 5 3 1

Selection and arrangement copyright © Helen Exley 1999
The moral right of the author has been asserted.

Written by William Shakespeare (1564-1616)
Words and pictures selected by Helen Exley
Picture research by Image Select International
Printed in China

www.hallmark.com

SHAKESPEARE
on Love

GIFT BOOKS
from Hallmark

SELECTED FOR HALLMARK BY HELEN EXLEY

BOK 4063

... WHEN LOVE SPEAKS,
THE VOICE OF ALL THE GODS
MAKE HEAVEN
DROWSY WITH THE HARMONY.

"LOVE'S LABOUR'S LOST", IV:III

O, but for my love,
day would turn to night!

"LOVE'S LABOUR'S LOST", IV:III

HOT BLOOD BEGETS
HOT THOUGHTS,
AND HOT THOUGHTS
BEGET HOT DEEDS,
AND HOT DEEDS IS LOVE.

"TROILUS AND CRESSIDA", III:1

It will set the heart on fire

Madam, you have bereft me of all words.

Only my blood speaks to you in my veins.

"The Merchant of Venice", III:ii

Affection is a coal that must be cooled,

Else, suffered, it will set the heart on fire.

The sea hath bounds, but deep desire hath none.

"Venus and Adonis", lines 387-389

ONE TURF SHALL SERVE AS PILLOW
FOR US BOTH;
ONE HEART, ONE BED; TWO BOSOMS,
AND ONE TROTH.

"A MIDSUMMER NIGHT'S DREAM", II:II

... my heart unto yours is knit,
So that but one heart we can make of it....

"A MIDSUMMER NIGHT'S DREAM", II:11

EXPECTATION WHIRLS ME ROUND

I am giddy. Expectation whirls me round.
Th'imaginary relish is so sweet
That it enchants my sense.

"TROILUS AND CRESSIDA", III:II

So tedious is this day
As is the night before some festival
To an impatient child that hath new robes
And may not wear them.

"ROMEO AND JULIET", III:II

... I WILL WEAR MY HEART UPON MY SLEEVE.

"OTHELLO", I.I

For such as I am, all true lovers are,
Unstaid and skittish in all motions else
Save in the constant image of the creature
That is beloved.

"TWELFTH NIGHT", II:IV

Your brother and my sister no sooner met but they looked; no sooner looked but they loved; no sooner loved but they sighed; no sooner sighed but they asked one another the reason; no sooner knew the reason but they sought the remedy.

"AS YOU LIKE IT", V:II

"Who ever loved that loved not at first sight?"

"AS YOU LIKE IT", III:V

EVEN SO QUICKLY
MAY ONE CATCH THE PLAGUE?

"TWELFTH NIGHT", I:V

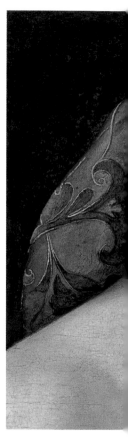

ETERNITY WAS IN OUR LIPS AND EYES,
BLISS IN OUR BROWS' BENT.

"ANTONY AND CLEOPATRA", I:III

AFTER HIM I LOVE

MORE THAN I LOVE THESE EYES, MORE THAN MY LIFE,

MORE BY ALL MORES....

"TWELFTH NIGHT", V:1

A LOVER'S EYES WILL GAZE
AN EAGLE BLIND

But love, first learnèd in a lady's eyes,
Lives not alone immurèd in the brain,
But with the motion of all elements
Courses as swift as thought in every power,
And gives to every power a double power
Above their functions and their offices.
It adds a precious seeing to the eye –
A lover's eyes will gaze an eagle blind.
A lover's ear will hear the lowest sound.

"Love's Labour's Lost", IV:III

... IS NOT LOVE A HERCULES,

STILL CLIMBING TREES IN THE HESPERIDES?

SUBTLE AS SPHINX; AS SWEET AND MUSICAL

AS BRIGHT APOLLO'S LUTE

STRUNG WITH HIS HAIR.

"LOVE'S LABOUR'S LOST", IV:III

SEE WHERE SHE COMES, APPARELLED LIKE THE SPRING

See where she comes, apparelled
like the spring,
Graces her subjects, and her thoughts
the king
Of ev'ry virtue gives renown to men;
Her face the book of praises,
where is read
Nothing but curious pleasures,
as from thence
Sorrow were ever razed and
testy wrath
Could never be her mild companion.

"PERICLES", I:1

My bounty is as boundless as the sea,
My love as deep. the more I give to thee
The more I have, for both are infinite.

"Romeo and Juliet", II:1

The brightness of her cheek would shame those stars
As daylight doth a lamp; her eye in heaven
Would through the airy region stream so bright
That birds would sing and think it were not night.

"ROMEO AND JULIET", II:1

DOUBT THOU THE STARS ARE FIRE,
DOUBT THAT THE SUN DOTH MOVE;
DOUBT TRUTH TO BE A LIAR,
BUT NEVER DOUBT I LOVE.

"HAMLET", II:II

Shall I command thy love? I may.
Shall I enforce thy love? I could.
Shall I entreat thy love? I will.

"LOVE'S LABOUR'S LOST", IV:1

For where thou art, there is the world itself.

"HENRY VI", PART II, III:iii

Lady, as you are mine, I am yours.
I give away myself for you, and dote
upon the exchange.

"MUCH ADO ABOUT NOTHING", II:1

O, she doth teach the torches to burn bright!
It seems she hangs upon the cheek of night
As a rich jewel in an Ethiope's ear —
Beauty too rich for use, for earth too dear!

"ROMEO AND JULIET", I:V

VALENTINE: Why, how know you that I am in love?

SPEED: Marry, by these special marks: first, you have learned... to wreathe your arms, like a malcontent; to relish a love-song, like a robin redbreast; to walk alone, like one that had the pestilence; to sigh, like a schoolboy that had lost his ABC; to weep, like a young wench that had buried her grandam; to fast, like one that takes diet; to watch, like one that fears robbing; to speak puling, like a beggar at Hallowmas....

And now you are metamorphosed with a mistress, that when I look on you I can hardly think you my master.

"THE TWO GENTLEMEN OF VERONA", II:1

WHY, HOW KNOW YOU THAT I AM IN LOVE?

SOVEREIGN OF SIGHS AND GROANS

This wimpled, whining, purblind, wayward boy,
This Signor Junior, giant dwarf, Dan Cupid,
Regent of love-rhymes, lord of folded arms,
Th'anointed sovereign of sighs and groans,
Liege of all loiterers and malcontents,
Dread prince of plackets, king of codpieces,
Sole imperator and great general
Of trotting paritors – O my little heart!
And I to be a corporal of his field,
And wear his colours like a tumbler's hoop!

"LOVE'S LABOUR'S LOST", III:I

... HOW TO KNOW A MAN IN LOVE

ROSALIND [AS GANYMEDE]: [My uncle] taught me how to know a man in love, in which cage of rushes I am sure you are not prisoner.

ORLANDO: What were his marks?

ROSALIND: A lean cheek, which you have not; a blue eye and sunken, which you have not; an unquestionable spirit, which you have not; a beard neglected, which you have not... then your hose should be ungartered, your bonnet unbanded, your sleeve unbuttoned, your shoe untied, and everything about you demonstrating a careless desolation.

"AS YOU LIKE IT", III:II

As love is full of unbefitting strains,
All wanton as a child, skipping and vain.

"LOVE'S LABOUR'S LOST", V:II

LOVE IS BLIND

Thou, Julia, thou hast metamorphosed me,
Made me neglect my studies, lose my time,
War with good counsel, set the world at naught;
Made wit with musing weak, heart sick with thought.

"THE TWO GENTLEMEN OF VERONA", I:I

... love is blind, and lovers cannot see
The pretty follies that themselves commit.

"THE MERCHANT OF VENICE", II:VI

LOVE IS MERELY A MADNESS

Love is merely a madness,
and I tell you, deserves as well a dark house
and a whip as madmen do.

"AS YOU LIKE IT", III:II

If thou rememberest not the slightest folly
That ever love did make thee run into,
Thou hast not loved.

"AS YOU LIKE IT", II:IV

Love looks not with the eyes, but with the mind,
And therefore is winged Cupid painted blind.

"A MIDSUMMER NIGHT'S DREAM", I:I

I do much wonder that one man, seeing how much
another man is a fool when he dedicates his behaviours
to love, will, after he hath laughed at such shallow
follies in others, become the argument of his own
scorn by falling in love.

"MUCH ADO ABOUT NOTHING", II:III

IF MUSIC BE THE FOOD OF LOVE

If music be the food of love, play on,

Give me excess of it that, surfeiting,

The appetite may sicken and so die.

That strain again, it had a dying fall.

Oh, it came o'er my ear like the sweet sound

That breathes upon a bank of violets,

Stealing and giving odour.

"TWELFTH NIGHT", I.I

LOVE THAT COMES TOO LATE

... love that comes too late,
Like a remorseful pardon slowly carried,
To the grace-sender turns a sour offence,
Crying, "That's good that's gone."

"All's Well That Ends Well", V.iii

If ever — as that ever may be near —
You meet in some fresh cheek the power of fancy,
Then shall you know the wounds invisible
That love's keen arrows make.

"As You Like It", III:v

This love will undo us all.

"TROILUS AND CRESSIDA", III:I

By heaven, I do love, and it hath taught me to rhyme and to be melancholy.

"LOVE'S LABOUR'S LOST", IV:III

Love is a smoke made with the fume of sighs,

Being purged, a fire sparkling in lovers' eyes,

Being vexed, a sea nourished with lovers' tears.

What is it else? A madness most discreet,

A choking gall and a preserving sweet.

"ROMEO AND JULIET", I:1

The course of true love never did run smooth.

"A MIDSUMMER NIGHT'S DREAM", I:1

LOVE GOES TOWARD LOVE

AS SCHOOLBOYS

FROM THEIR BOOKS,

BUT LOVE FROM LOVE,

TOWARD SCHOOL

WITH HEAVY LOOKS.

"ROMEO AND JULIET", II:1

O, learn to read what silent love hath writ!
To hear with eyes belongs to love's fine wit.

'Twere all one
That I should love a bright particular star
And think to wed it, he is so above me.
In his bright radiance and collateral light
Must I be comforted, not in his sphere.
Th'ambition in my love thus plagues itself.
The hind that would be mated by the lion
Must die for love.

"ALL'S WELL THAT ENDS WELL", I:I

WITH SIGNS OF FIRE

OLIVIA: How does he love me?
VIOLA: With adorations, fertile tears,
With groans that thunder love,
  with sighs of fire.

"TWELFTH NIGHT", I:V

They are in the very wrath of love,
  and they will together. Clubs cannot part them.

"AS YOU LIKE IT", V:II

Never durst poet touch a pen to write

Until his ink were tempered with love's sighs.

O, then his lines would ravish savage ears,

And plant in tyrants mild humility.

MY LIPS,
TWO BLUSHING PILGRIMS

ROMEO: If I profane with my unworthiest hand

This holy shrine, the gentler sin is this:

My lips, two blushing pilgrims, ready stand

To smooth that rough touch with a tender kiss.

JULIET: Good pilgrim, you do wrong your hand too much,

Which mannerly devotion shows in this;

For saints have hands that pilgrims' hands do touch,

And palm to palm is holy palmers' kiss.

ROMEO: Have not saints lips, and holy palmers, too?

JULIET: Ay, pilgrim, lips that they must use in prayer.

ROMEO: O then, dear saint, let lips do what hands do:

They pray; grant thou, lest faith turn to despair.

JULIET: Saints do not move, though grant for prayers'

sake.

ROMEO: Then move not while my prayer's effect I take.

(*He kisses her*)

Thus from my lips, by thine my sin is purged.

JULIET: Then have my lips the sin that they have took.

ROMEO: Sin from my lips? O trespass sweetly urged!

Give me my sin again.

(*He kisses her*)

JULIET: You kiss by th'book.

How silver-sweet sound lovers' tongues by night,
Like softest music to attending ears!

"ROMEO AND JULIET", II:1

Good night, good night. Parting is such sweet sorrow
That I shall say good night till it be morrow.

"ROMEO AND JULIET", II:1

Yon light is not daylight; I know it

JULIET: Wilt thou be gone? It is not yet near day.
It was the nightingale, and not the lark,
That pierced the fear-full hollow of thine ear.
Nightly she sings on yon pom'granate tree.
Believe me, love, it was the nightingale.
ROMEO: It was the lark, the herald of the morn,
No nightingale. Look, love, what envious streaks
Do lace the severing clouds in yonder east.
Night's candles are burnt out, and jocund day
Stands tiptoe on the misty mountain tops.
I must be gone and live, or stay and die.
JULIET: Yon light is not daylight; I know it, I.
It is some meteor that the sun exhaled

To be to thee this night a torchbearer
And light thee on thy way to Mantua.
Therefore stay yet. Thou need'st not to be gone.
ROMEO: Let me be ta'en, let me be put to death.
I am content, so thou wilt have it so.
I'll say yon grey is not the morning's eye.
'Tis but the pale reflex of Cynthia's brow;
Nor that is not the lark whose notes do beat
The vaulty heaven so high above our heads.
I have more care to stay than will to go.

"ROMEO AND JULIET", III:v

TAKE HIM
AND CUT HIM OUT IN LITTLE STARS,
AND HE WILL MAKE THE FACE
OF HEAVEN SO FINE
THAT ALL THE WORLD
WILL BE IN LOVE WITH NIGHT
AND PAY NO WORSHIP
TO THE GARISH SUN.

"ROMEO AND JULIET", III:II

Love comforteth, like sunshine after rain,
But lust's effect is tempest after sun.
Love's gentle spring doth always fresh remain;
Lust's winter comes ere summer half be done.

"VENUS AND ADONIS", LINES 799-802

MEN WERE DECEIVERS EVER...

Young men's love then lies
Not truly in their hearts, but in their eyes.

"ROMEO AND JULIET", II:II

Sigh no more, ladies, sigh no more.
Men were deceivers ever.
One foot in sea, and one on shore,
To one thing constant never.
Then sigh not so, but let them go,
And be you blithe and bonny,
Converting all your sounds of woe
Into hey nonny nonny.

The fraud of men was ever so
Since summer first was leafy.

"MUCH ADO ABOUT NOTHING", II:III

THE POOR SOUL SAT SIGHING by a sycamore tree,

Sing all a green willow.

Her hand on her bosom, her head on her knee,

Sing willow, willow, willow.

The fresh streams ran by her and murmured her moans,

Sing willow, willow, willow.

Her salt tears fell from her, and softened the stones,

Sing willow, willow, willow,

Sing all, a green willow must be my garland.

"OTHELLO", IV:III

War, death or sickness did lay seige to [love],

Making it momentary as a sound,

Swift as a shadow, short as any dream,

Brief as the lightning in the collied night,

That, in a spleen, unfolds both heaven and earth,

And, ere a man hath power to say "Behold!",

The jaws of darkness do devour it up.

So quick bright things come to confusion.

"A Midsummer Night's Dream", I:I

I know I love in vain, strive against hope;

Yet in this captious and intenable sieve

I still pour in the waters of my love

And lack not to lose still.

"All's Well That Ends Well", I:III

AGAINST THAT TIME...
WHEN I SHALL SEE THEE FROWN
ON MY DEFECTS

Against that time, if ever that time come,

When I shall see thee frown on my defects,

When as thy love hath cast his utmost sum,

Call'd to that audit by advis'd respects;

Against that time when thou shalt strangely pass

And scarcely greet me with that sun, thine eye,

When love, converted from the thing it was,

Shall reasons find of settled gravity –

Against that time do I ensconce me here

Within the knowledge of mine own desert,

And this my hand against myself uprear,

To guard the lawful reasons on thy part:

To leave poor me thou hast the strength of laws,

Since why to love I can allege no cause.

SONNET 49

Ruin hath taught me thus to ruminate —
That Time will come and take my love away.
This thought is as a death, which cannot choose
But weep to have that which it fears to lose.

FROM SONNET 64

[Women's eyes] sparkle still the right

Promethean fire;

They are the books, the arts, the academes

That show, contain, and nourish all the world,

else none at all in aught

proves excellent.

Down on your knees,
And thank heaven,
fasting, for a good man's love.

"As You Like It", III:v

To die is to be banished from myself,
And Silvia is my self. Banished from her
Is self from self, a deadly banishment.
What light is light, if Silvia be not seen?
What joy is joy, if Silvia be not by —
Unless it be to think that she is by,
And feed upon the shadow of perfection,

EXCEPT I BE BY SILVIA
IN THE NIGHT
THERE IS NO MUSIC
IN THE NIGHTINGALE

Except I be by Silvia in the night
There is no music in the nightingale.
Unless I look on Silvia in the day
There is no day for me to look upon.
She is my essence, and I leave to be
If I be not by her fair influence
Fostered, illumined, cherished, kept alive.

"THE TWO GENTLEMEN OF VERONA", III:1

When in disgrace with Fortune and men's eyes,
I all alone beweep my outcast state,
And trouble deaf heaven with my bootless cries,
And look upon myself, and curse my fate,
Wishing me like to one more rich in hope,
Featur'd like him, like him with friends possess'd,
Desiring this man's art, and that man's scope,
With what I most enjoy contented least;
Yet in these thoughts myself almost despising,
Haply I think on thee, and then my state,
Like to the lark at break of day arising
From sullen earth, sings hymns at heaven's gate;
For thy sweet love rememb'red such wealth brings
That then I scorn to change my state with kings.

ALL DAYS ARE NIGHTS TO SEE TILL I SEE THEE

When most I wink, then do mine eyes best see,

For all the day they view things unrespected;

But when I sleep, in dreams they look on thee,

And, darkly bright, are bright in dark directed;

Then thou whose shadow shadows doth make bright,

How would thy shadow's form form happy show

To the clear day with thy much clearer light,

When to unseeing eyes thy shade shines so!

How would, I say, mine eyes be blessed made

By looking on thee in the living day,

When in dead night thy fair imperfect shade

Through heavy sleep on sightless eyes doth stay!

All days are nights to see till I see thee,

And nights bright days when dreams do show thee me.

SONNET 43

My imagination

Carries no favour in't but Bertram's.

I am undone. There is no living, none,

If Bertram be away....

'Twas pretty, though a plague,

To see him every hour, to sit and draw

His archèd brows, his hawking eye, his curls,

In our heart's table – heart too capable

Of every line and trick of his sweet favour.

But now he's gone, and my idolatrous fancy

Must sanctify his relics.

"ALL'S WELL THAT ENDS WELL", I:1

Being your slave, what should I do but tend

Upon the hours and times of your desire?

I have no precious time at all to spend,

Nor services to do, till you require.

Nor dare I chide the world-without-end hour,

Whilst I, my sovereign, watch the clock for you,

Nor think the bitterness of absence sour,

When you have bid your servant once adieu;

Nor dare I question with my jealous thought

Where you may be, or your affairs suppose,

But, like a sad slave, stay and think of nought

Save where you are how happy you make those.

So true a fool is love that in your will,

Though you do anything, he thinks no ill.

SONNET 57

WHILST I, MY SOVEREIGN,
WATCH THE CLOCK FOR YOU...

FROM YOU HAVE I BEEN ABSENT
IN THE SPRING

From you have I been absent in the spring,
When proud-pied April, dress'd in all his trim,
Hath put a spirit of youth in every thing,
That heavy Saturn laugh'd and leap'd with him.
Yet nor the lays of birds, nor the sweet smell
Of different flowers in odour and in hue,
Could make me any summer's story tell,
Or from their proud lap pluck them where they grew;
Nor did I wonder at the lily's white,
Nor praise the deep vermilion in the rose:
They were but sweet, but figures of delight,
Drawn after you, you pattern of all those.
Yet seem'd it winter still, and, you away,
As with your shadow I with these did play.

SONNET 98

O, NEVER SAY THAT I WAS FALSE OF HEART,

Though absence seem'd my flame to qualify!

As easy might I from my self depart

As from my soul, which in thy breast doth lie:

That is my home of love. If I have rang'd,

Like him that travels, I return again,

Just to the time, not with the time exchang'd,

So that my self bring water for my stain.

Never believe, though in my nature reign'd

All frailties that besiege all kinds of blood,

That it could so preposterously be stain'd

To leave for nothing all thy sum of good;

For nothing this wide universe I call,

Save thou, my rose; in it thou art my all.

How like a winter hath my absence been
From thee, the pleasure of the fleeting year!
What freezings have I felt, what dark days seen!
What old December's bareness everywhere!...

For summer and his pleasures wait on thee,
And, thou away, the very birds are mute;
Or, if they sing, 'tis with so dull a cheer
That leaves look pale, dreading the winter's near.

FROM SONNET 97

LET ME NOT
TO THE MARRIAGE OF TRUE MINDS
ADMIT IMPEDIMENTS

Let me not to the marriage of true minds

Admit impediments. Love is not love

Which alters when it alteration finds,

Or bends with the remover to remove.

O no! it is an ever-fixed mark,

That looks on tempests and is never shaken;

It is the star to every wand'ring bark,

Whose worth's unknown, although his height be taken.

Love's not Time's fool, though rosy lips and cheeks

Within his bending sickle's compass come;

Love alters not with his brief hours and weeks,

But bears it out even to the edge of doom.

If this be error, and upon me prov'd,

I never writ, nor no man ever lov'd.

SONNET 116

A GOOD HEART, KATE, IS THE SUN AND THE MOON...

... dear Kate, take a fellow of plain and uncoined
constancy, for he perforce must do thee
right, because he hath not the gift to woo in other
places. For these fellows of infinite tongue,
that can rhyme themselves into ladies' favours, they do
always reason themselves out again. What! A speaker is
but a prater, a rhyme is but a ballad; a good leg
will fall, a straight back will stoop, a black beard will
turn white, a curled pate will grow bald, a
fair face will wither, a full eye will wax hollow, but a
good heart, Kate, is the sun and the moon – or rather
the sun and not the moon, for it shines bright
and never changes, but keeps his course truly.

"HENRY V", V:II

MY LIFE BE THINE

... our day of marriage shall be yours,
One feast, one house, one mutual happiness.

"THE TWO GENTLEMEN OF VERONA", V:IV

My house, mine honour, yea my life be thine.

"ALL'S WELL THAT ENDS WELL", IV:II

But when this ring
Parts from this finger, then parts life
from hence;
O, then be bold to say Bassanio's dead!

"THE MERCHANT OF VENICE", III:II

Let those who are in favour with their stars
Of public honour and proud titles boast,
Whilst I, whom fortune of such triumph bars,
Unlook'd for joy in that I honour most.
Great princes' favourites their fair leaves spread
But as the marigold at the sun's eye;
And in themselves their pride lies buried,
For at a frown they in their glory die.
The painful warrior famoused for fight,
After a thousand victories once foil'd,
Is from the book of honour razed quite,
And all the rest forgot for which he toil'd.
    Then happy I, that love and am beloved
    Where I may not remove nor be removed.

SONNET 25

THEN HAPPY I,
THAT LOVE AND AM BELOVED

Not marble nor the gilded monuments
Of princes shall outlive this pow'rful rhyme;
But you shall shine more bright in these contents
Than unswept stone, besmear'd with sluttish time.
When wasteful war shall statues overturn,
And broils root out the work of masonry,
Nor Mars his sword nor war's quick fire shall burn
The living record of your memory.
'Gainst death and all-oblivious enmity
Shall you pace forth; your praise shall still find room,
Even in the eyes of all posterity
That wear this world out to the ending doom.
So, till the judgment that yourself arise,
You live in this, and dwell in lovers' eyes.

SONNET 55

... WERE I CROWNED
THE MOST IMPERIAL MONARCH,
THEREOF MOST WORTHY,
WERE I THE FAIREST YOUTH
THAT EVER MADE EYE SWERVE,
HAD FORCE AND KNOWLEDGE
MORE THAN WAS EVER MAN'S,
I WOULD NOT PRIZE THEM
WITHOUT HER LOVE.

"THE WINTER'S TALE", IV:IV

AS TRUE AS STEEL

TROILUS: True swains in love shall in the world to come
Approve their truth by Troilus. When their rhymes,
Full of protest, of oath and big compare,
Wants similes, truth tired with iteration –
"As true as steel, as plantage to the moon,
As sun to day, as turtle to her mate,
As iron to adamant, as earth to th'centre" –
Yet, after all comparisons of truth,
As truth's authentic author to be cited,
"As true as Troilus" shall crown up the verse
And sanctify the numbers.

CRESSIDA: Prophet may you be!
If I be false, or swerve a hair from truth,
When time is old and hath forgot itself,
When water drops have worn the stones of Troy
And blind oblivion swallowed cities up,
And mighty states characterless are grated
To dusty nothing, yet let memory
From false to false among false maids in love
Upbraid my falsehood. When they've said, "as false
As air, as water, wind or sandy earth,
As fox to lamb, or wolf to heifer's calf,
Pard to the hind, or stepdame to her son",
Yea, let them say, to stick the heart of falsehood,
"As false as Cressid".

"TROILUS AND CRESSIDA", III:II

SHALL I COMPARE THEE TO A SUMMER'S DAY?

Shall I compare thee to a summer's day?

Thou art more lovely and more temperate.

Rough winds do shake the darling buds of May,

And summer's lease hath all too short a date:

Sometime too hot the eye of heaven shines,

And often is his gold complexion dimm'd;

And every fair from fair some time declines,

By chance, or nature's changing course, untrimm'd;

But thy eternal summer shall not fade

Nor lose possession of that fair thou ow'st;

Nor shall Death brag thou wand'rest in his shade,

When in eternal lines to time thou grow'st.

So long as men can breathe or eyes can see,

So long lives this, and this gives life to thee.

SONNET 18

Is whispering nothing?

Is leaning cheek to cheek? Is meeting noses?

Kissing with inside lip? Stopping the career

Of laughter with a sigh? – a note infallible

Of breaking honesty. Horsing foot on foot?

Skulking in corners? Wishing clocks more swift,

Hours minutes, noon midnight? And all eyes

Blind with the pin and web but theirs, theirs only,

That would unseen be wicked? Is this nothing?

Why then the world and all that's in't is nothing,

The covering sky is nothing, Bohemia nothing,

My wife is nothing, nor nothing have these nothings

If this be nothing.

"THE WINTER'S TALE", I:II

IF THIS BE NOTHING

A CLOUD TAKES ALL AWAY

O, how this spring of love resembleth
The uncertain glory of an April day,
Which now shows all the beauty of the sun,
And by and by a cloud takes all away.

"THE TWO GENTLEMEN OF VERONA", I:III

... Still with me

So, either by thy picture or my love,
Thyself away thou art present still with me;
For thou not farther than my thoughts canst move,
And I am still with them, and they with thee....

FROM SONNET 47

List of illustrations